# The Wonder of God's World
# Sound

by
## Bonita Searle-Barnes

Illustrated by Colin Smithson

A LION BOOK

Text by Bonita Searle-Barnes
Copyright © 1993 Lion
Publishing
Illustrations copyright ©
1993 Colin Smithson

Published by
**Lion Publishing**
850 North Grove Avenue,
Elgin, Illinois 60120, USA
ISBN 0 7459 2692 4

First edition 1993
Reprinted 1994

**Acknowledgments**
Photographs by Lion
Publishing: spread 10; Oxford
Scientific Films/Doug Allan:
spread 1 (right)/Stephen
Dalton: spread 5/Hermann
Eisenbeiss: spread 2/E.
Lauber: spread 14/Kjell B.
Sandver: spread 7; Zefa (UK)
Ltd: cover, spreads 1 (left), 3,
4, 6

Library of Congress CIP Data
applied for

Printed and bound in
Singapore

# Sound... and a whole lot more!

Children love finding out about the world they live in. This book provides loads of activities to help them find out about sound. They can have hours of fun listening to different sounds and noting their discoveries. In this way, they will learn the basic skills of scientific research.

- *More* They can also find out about some of the things that can be done with sound: making it louder or softer, making it travel farther or stopping it so it isn't a bother.

- *More* Throughout the ages, children, poets, musicians, and some of the world's greatest scientists have thrilled to the wonder of the natural world: the variety, the beauty. Although a book can't make sounds, the photos in this book are a starting point to help children find out what makes the many different sounds that fill the world with delight: birds, animals . . . even plants! The activities themselves help children explore the variety of sounds more directly, by listening for different notes, different rhythms, different voices.

- *More* This book helps them, too, to find words to express the excitement and joy in it all. Learning new words is a vital part of exploring the world, and a key to communicating with other people.

- *More* This book also provides an opportunity to explore the rich heritage of poems and songs that people have written to celebrate their world. It draws, for example, on psalms from the Bible, which have been used for centuries to say thank you to the God who made the world.

- *More* There is the question, too, of the feelings that people link with sounds: music evokes different moods, as do different musical instruments. How do children respond to loud noises? How do they feel about silence? Here is a perfect opportunity to encourage and reassure them.

This book is intended to give a very broad approach to exploring sound, that will enrich your children's total understanding of their world. You'll be surprised at what you discover, too, as you explore the world as a child do

# Welcome to the laboratory of the world!

Sound is all around you: at this moment you may be able to hear the sound of people chattering and laughing, machines working, music playing.

If you keep very quiet, you may hear other sounds: people breathing, birds singing, the breeze rustling in the leaves.

Imagine a world that was completely silent: no music, no laughter, no singing. You would not be able to use words to share your news and say what things made you happy and what things made you sad. How different everything would be!

But *why* is there sound? The 'why' questions are always the hardest! The most famous book in the world, the Bible, says that God made the world the way it is, as a wonderful home for all living things, for people to take care of and to enjoy. Sound is part of the Designer's plan for the world.

# Contents

# ▶ 1 Sounds

What sounds can you hear around you now? Close your eyes and think only about what you can hear.

The world is full of different sounds.

People and animals have been designed with voices to make sounds, and ears to hear them. They can use sounds to send each other messages.

They can hear what is going on around them, and so avoid danger.

Some sounds are just fun to listen to.

Find out more about the way sound is designed to work. Then you can make it work for you.

**Spring song**

*When the winter rains have stopped*
*You'll see the flowers of spring*
*The sound of birds is everywhere*
*The whole world seems to sing.*

**From the Song of Songs, in the Bible**

Some birds sing several notes one after the other, like a little tune. Listen carefully for the tunes that birds sing. Listen to them trilling, chirruping, warbling, fluting. Can you sing like a bird?

Have you ever thought about the sounds plants make?

# Forest in the city

Listen for the sound of the wind rustling plants and leaves.

Try rustling different types of paper to make the sounds of the wind in the leaves and branches. What gives the best effects?

- Cut out leaves from different sorts of paper and thread them together to make a mobile.
- Hang it where it will catch the breeze and make forest sounds for you—wherever you live.

# ▶ 2 Making waves

Sounds happen when something shakes the air, making little waves that spread outwards.

Try these experiments.

## Water waves

- Find a large bucket and fill it halfway up with water.
- Now drop a pebble in.
- What happens to the surface of the water? Draw a picture of what you see.

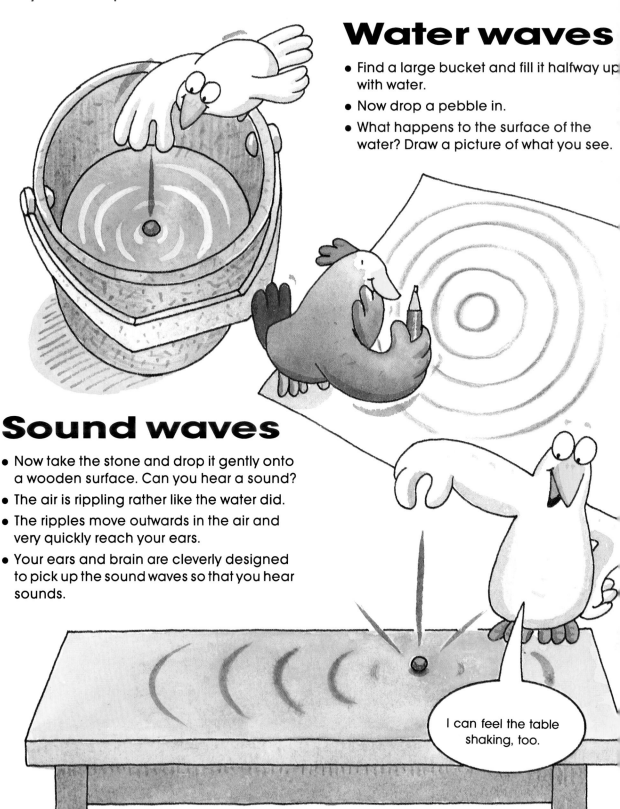

## Sound waves

- Now take the stone and drop it gently onto a wooden surface. Can you hear a sound?
- The air is rippling rather like the water did.
- The ripples move outwards in the air and very quickly reach your ears.
- Your ears and brain are cleverly designed to pick up the sound waves so that you hear sounds.

I can feel the table shaking, too.

# Water words

The pond skater walks across the surface of water. It makes ripples as it travels. Pond skaters can use ripple patterns to send messages to each other.

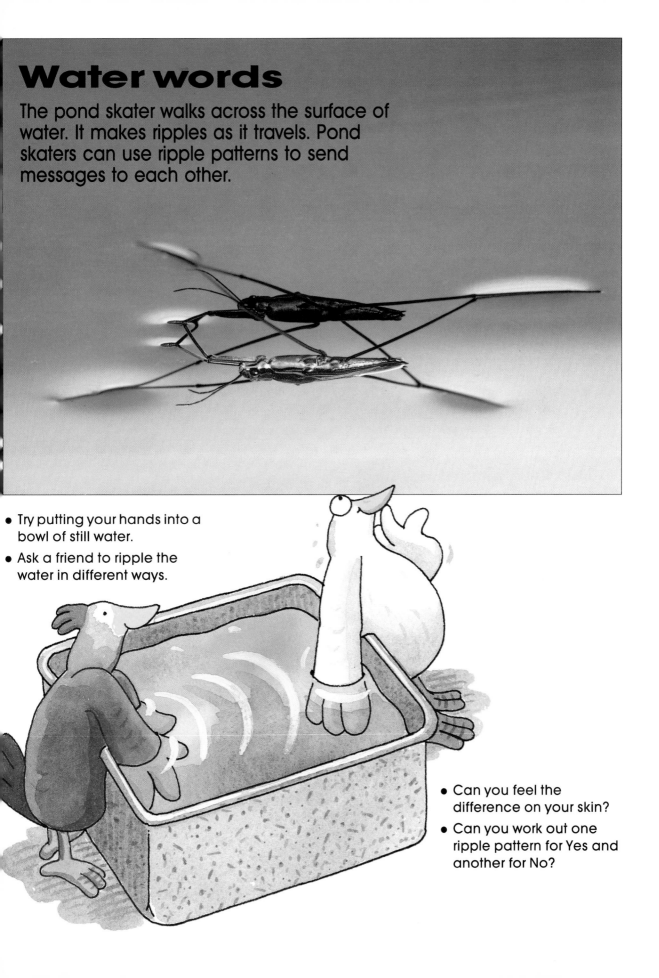

- Try putting your hands into a bowl of still water.
- Ask a friend to ripple the water in different ways.

- Can you feel the difference on your skin?
- Can you work out one ripple pattern for Yes and another for No?

# ▶ 3 Silence

Sounds soon spread out from whatever made them.

The farther you are away from a sound, the quieter it will seem.

- How close do you have to be to another person for them to hear you talking?
- What happens if you move farther away and speak without raising your voice?
- What happens if you shout?

Stop!

Stop!

Stop!

# Muffled

Some things absorb the ripples made by sound.

Find a clock with a loud tick or with an alarm you can set.

- How loud is the noise normally?
- What does it sound like if you put it under a cushion?
- What does it sound like in a cardboard box?
- Try wrapping the clock in different things to find out what blocks the sound best.
- How could you use your discoveries to block out the sound of noisy music?

Snow is like a giant blanket on the ground. It muffles sounds. Everywhere seems quieter in the snow.

# ush

How do you feel when everything around you is quiet?

Many people like to be alone sometimes, so that they can think.

Jesus, the founder of Christianity, liked to be alone so he could talk and listen to God. He told his followers to spend time alone so they could pray to God too.

It's nice to sit quietly and think.

*Thank you for the world so sweet*
*Thank you for the food we eat*
*Thank you for the birds that sing*
*Thank you, God, for everything.*

# ▶ 4 Can you hear me?

Birds are cleverly designed with ears you can't see!

We know that there are sounds because we hear them.

Look at animals with big ears. The special design of their ears helps them to pick up even the slightest sound waves, so they can escape from danger.

## Big ears

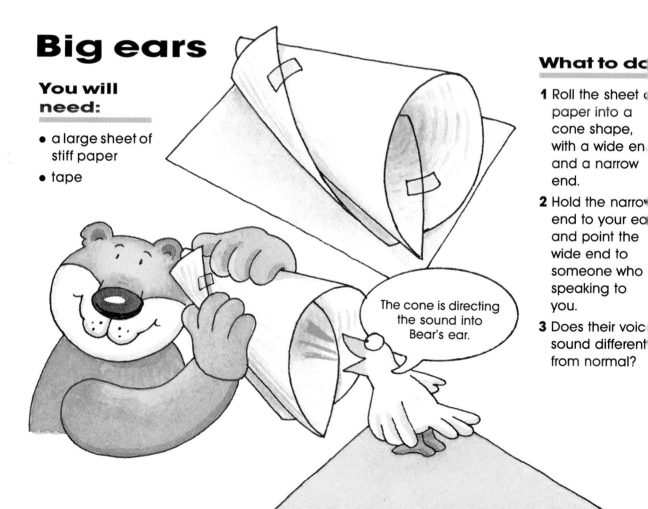

### You will need:

- a large sheet of stiff paper
- tape

The cone is directing the sound into Bear's ear.

### What to do

1 Roll the sheet of paper into a cone shape, with a wide end and a narrow end.

2 Hold the narrow end to your ear and point the wide end to someone who speaking to you.

3 Does their voice sound different from normal?

# Speak up

Use your paper cone to make your voice sound louder. Just speak into the narrow end.

# ▶ 5 Echoes

Have you ever heard an echo? An echo is a sound that comes back to you.

Just as a ball bounces off a wall, sounds bounce back to you off hard surfaces.

Try shouting at a wall of rock, or tall building, or when you are standing under a bridge.

# Batty ideas

Special designs for every kind of creature.

Bats use echoes to find their way around. They make little squeaks that echo off hard objects. They are able to work out where things are from the way the echo comes back to them. That is how they hunt for the moths they feed on.

The world is full of clever designs to copy.

A brilliant way of finding things in the dark!

# Echoes under the sea

People can also use echoes to help them find things, but they need a machine to help them. This machine sends out sound waves and measures how long they take to bounce back. People on fishing boats use echo sounders to find out where there are shoals of fish under the water.

# ▶ 6 Near and far

Some storms have thunder and lightning.

The flash of hot lightning makes the air move so fast that it makes a loud bang.

This is thunder.

I usually see lightning before I hear thunder.

Thunder and lightning happen at the same time. But if you are far away from where they happen, the sound and the light have to travel to get where you are.

Light travels faster, so it gets there first.

Sound travels more slowly, so you hear it later.

# Hide and seek

ay hide and seek with a friend, but give the
erson hiding a shaker or a whistle.
When they are in their hiding place, they
ake a noise.
How good are you at finding where they
re by listening to where the sound is coming
om?

# Bang

o loud noises make you jump?
How do you feel when you hear
under?
Here is a prayer that people can
ay to God when they are afraid.

*Please, God,
help me to be brave and strong
and take my fear away.*

**From Psalm 27 of the Bible**

# ▶ 7 Footsteps

Think of the sounds living creatures make as they move:

the pitter-patter of a mouse scampering;
the thundering sound of horses galloping.

## Hands and feet

- What sound do your shoes make when you walk on a soft carpet?
- What is different if you walk on a hard floor?
- Try walking on different surfaces in different shoes. Listen to the sounds they make.
- Which make the loudest noises—shoes with soft soles or shoes with hard soles?

- Now try clapping your hands. What sound do they make?
- How does the sound change if you wear gloves?

# Let's dance

...nd shoes that make a nice tap when you
...ove, and make sounds with your hands
...nd your feet.

...People dance when they are happy. Below
...a happy song from the Bible that talks
...bout dancing.

1. Take 3 steps forwards and clap your hands.

2. Take 3 steps backwards and clap your hands.

3. Step, hop 4 times in a circle.

4. Take 3 steps to the left and hop.

5. Take 3 steps to the right and hop.

6. Right hand to left knee, left hand to right knee.

7. Right hand to left heel, left hand to right heel.

*Hooray for God, who made the world,*
*Hooray for God the King.*
*Show him just how glad you are:*
*Play music, dance, and sing.*

**From Psalm 149 of the Bible**

# ►8 Fast and slow

## Rhythm band

Try making these musical instruments. Listen carefully to the different sounds they make.

Banging sounds are some of the easiest sounds to make. What you hit shakes the air— and that makes the noise.

Have you ever heard a woodpecker? It bangs its beak against the trunk of a tree, to make a hole in it to find insects to eat.

It bangs so fast that you hear a whirring sound.

How do different drumsticks affect the sound?

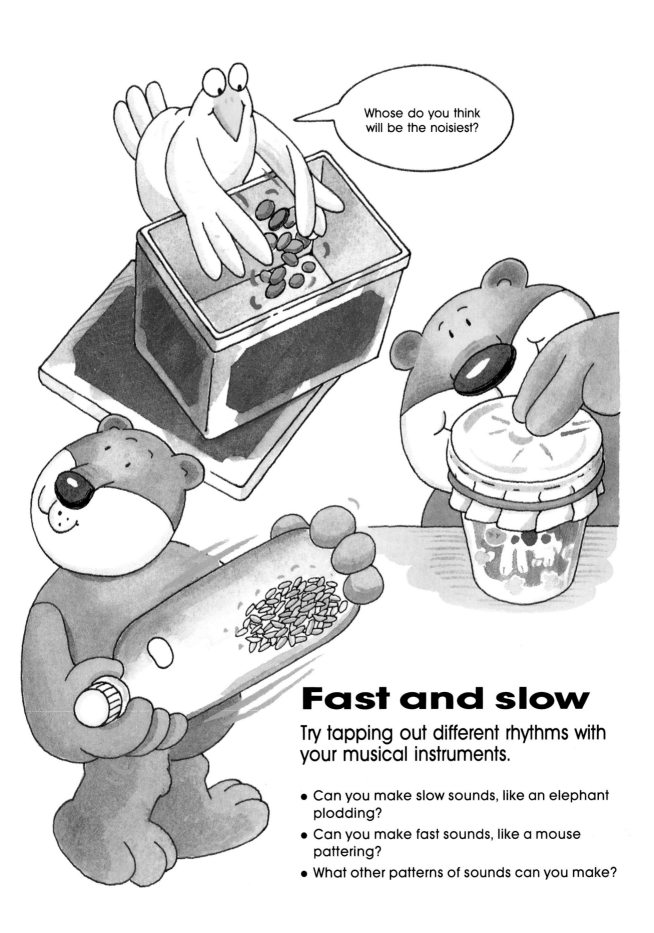

# Fast and slow

Try tapping out different rhythms with your musical instruments.

- Can you make slow sounds, like an elephant plodding?
- Can you make fast sounds, like a mouse pattering?
- What other patterns of sounds can you make?

# ▶9 High and low

Some sounds are high. Others are low.

## Whistling

Can you whistle?

**1** Make your lips into a small circle.

**2** Now blow gently through your lips. Move them slightly if you need to, to get sound.

- What happens if you blow hard? softly?
- Can you whistle high notes? low notes?
- Can you whistle a tune?

## Balloon trumpet

Blow up a balloon and stretch the neck sideways, allowing the air to escape in a narrow stream.

- What sound does the balloon make?
- Does the sound change if you make the air hole larger or smaller?

The balloon's whistling like you did!

# Musical chimes

Here is another way to make high notes and low notes.

## You will need:

- 8 drinking glasses
- a pitcher of water
- food coloring
- a teaspoon

To play a tune, you have to pick the high and low notes in the right order.

Some notes are long and some are short.

And some tunes are slow, but others are fast.

## What to do:

1. Add some food coloring to the water.
2. Pour some water into each glass. Put just a little in the first one, and a bit more in the next... and so on.
3. Tap each glass with the spoon. Listen to the different note each glass makes.
4. Try adding a bit more water or pouring some away until you have a nice row of notes.
5. Try playing a tune on the glasses!

# ► 10 Strings
## Wings and strings

Watch how strings move when you pluck them.

### You will need:

- a jam jar
- a rubber band

## What to do:

1 Stretch the rubber band over the jar.
2 Pluck it in the space above the opening.

- Can you see it moving backwards and forwards very fast?
- What sound does it make?
- What happens to the sound if you move the band so that the bit over the opening is more stretched?
- What happens if you give a gentle pluck? A strong pluck?
- How long does the note last? What happens to the sound if you pluck the string, and then touch it again gently?

Look at the way a butterfly moves its wings. Why do you think you can't hear a butterfly flapping?

# Zither

A zither is a traditional musical instrument. You can make a very simple zither.

## You will need:

- a loaf pan
- rubber bands of different thicknesses

## What to do:

1. Stretch the rubber bands around the pan, starting with the thickest one and ending with the thinnest.
2. Pluck each band and listen to the sound.
3. Try stretching the bands a bit more or a bit less over the opening to get the sound you like best.

You whistle it and I'll play it!

- Do you like the thin, pinging high notes?
- Or the deep, buzzing low notes?
- Can you make up a tune to play on your zither?
- Can you make up a happy tune?
- Can you make up a sad tune?

The zither is like a harp. Harps have been popular musical instruments for thousands of years. The Bible says that when the Israelite people were far from home and feeling sad, they wrote this poem:

*By the rivers of Babylon we sat down and wept when we remembered our home, Zion.*
*On the willows nearby*
*We hung up our harps,*
*Because we were too sad to sing.*

**From Psalm 137 of the Bible**

# ▶ 11 Your own set of strings

Your voice is very special. It does not sound like anyone else's. You can tell who is speaking to you simply by the sound of their voice.

## Voice parade

Listen to your family talking. Who has the highest voice? Who has the lowest voice?

# Voice show

What do you think a bear would sound like if it could talk? Can you make a voice like a bear?
What would a bird sound like?
Can you make up special talking voices for your toys? your pets?

What do you mean—'if' a bear could talk?

# Animal friends

Think of the sounds these animals make.
The Bible says that one day they will all be friends again. Imagine what sounds they might make then!

*One day the whole world will know*
*about God again.*
*The animals will be friends,*
*wolves and sheep, cows and bears,*
*and children will look after them.*

**From the book of Isaiah in the Bible**

# ▶ 12 Words

Words are wonderful things.
Some sound like what they mean.

Some are just fun to say.

HIPPOPOTAMUS

Some are hard to say in a rush.

Some groups of words begin with the same sound.

# Let's talk

It's great to have someone to talk to.
You can share the good things and the sad things that have happened to you.
You can say how you are feeling.
You can say kind words to make people feel happy.
Are these words kind or unkind?

I've got a present for Bear!

Come and play!

I had it first!

I'm going to go flying on Saturday!

Not too loud, please.

Your feathers are a mess!

# Kind words

Kind words make us feel loved and wanted.
Angry words make us sad.
The Bible says this about words:

*Do not use words that hurt people,
but only ones that help people,
the kind that encourage them
and do them good.*

**From the New Testament letter to the Ephesians**

# ▶13 Sing!

## Singing lesson

When you speak or sing, you use the vocal cords inside your throat. They are like folds of stretched skin. When air goes over them, they vibrate and make a sound, just as an elastic band makes a noise when you pluck it.

- Put your fingers on your throat and sing a low note.

- Can you feel the vibrations?

- Now sing a higher note. Do the vibrations change? How?

- Now sing the highest note you can. Is it easy? What happens to the vibrations now?

# Happy songs

Sometimes we are so happy that we want to sing. Here is a song that people sing to thank God for making the world.

All things bright and beautiful
All creatures great and small
All things wise and wonderful
The Lord God made them all.

He gave us eyes to see them
And lips that we might tell
How great is God Almighty
Who has made all things well.

**Mrs C. F. Alexander**

# 14 Sound sleuth

## What was that?

Our world is so noisy that we don't notice all the sounds around us.

   If you sit quietly, you may hear some of the quieter ones.

- Can you work out what they are?
- What can you hear right now?

ave you ever
eard seed pods
opping on a hot
ay at the end of
immer?

ver thought PLANTS
nade a noise . . .

# hear with my little ear

ere's a listening game to play. Listen for a sound, then
isk someone to guess what it is, by giving them just the
beginning letter of the word that describes it.

What noises beginning with B are in this picture?

I hear with my little
ear something
beginning with B.